Hockey's
TOP SCORERS

The SPORTS HEROES Library

Hockey's
TOP SCORERS

Richard Rainbolt

 Lerner Publications Company

Minneapolis

ACKNOWLEDGMENTS

The illustrations are reproduced through the courtesy of: pp. 6, 9, 11, 14, 17, 19, 22, 25, 28, 31, 33, 36, 39, 42, 44, 48, 50, 54, 56, 62, 66, 68, 69, 70, 71, David Bier Studios; p. 59, Club De Hockey Canadien, Incorporated.

LIBRARY OF CONGRESS CATALOGING IN PUBLICATION DATA

Rainbolt, Richard.
  Hockey's top scorers.

  (The Sports Heroes Library)
  SUMMARY: Brief biographies focusing on the careers of ten hockey stars: Maurice Richard, Ted Lindsay, Bernie Geoffrion, Jean Beliveau, Bobby Orr, Bobby Hull, Gordie Howe, Stan Mikita, Frank Mahovlich, and Phil Esposito.

  1. Hockey—Biography—Juvenile literature. [1. Hockey—Biography] I. Title.

GV848.5.A1R34   796.9′62′0922[B][920]   74-27471
ISBN 0-8225-1056-1

Published simultaneously in Canada by
J. M. Dent & Sons (Canada) Ltd., Don Mills, Ontario

Manufactured in the United States of America

International Standard Book Number: 0-8225-1056-1
Library of Congress Catalog Card Number: 74-27471

Contents

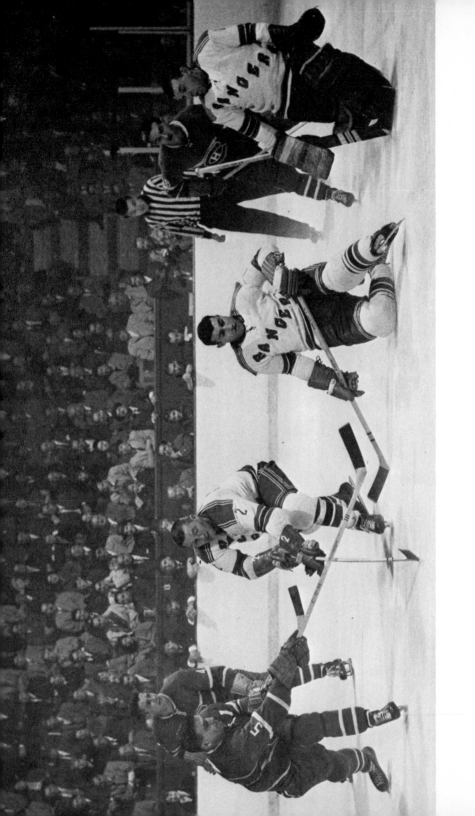

Until just a few years ago, professional hockey was watched mostly by Canadians. But the game is now winning fans in the United States, where many new teams have been established.

More Americans became interested in hockey after the expansion of the National Hockey League (NHL). Between 1967 and 1972, the NHL added 10 new teams. Nine of these teams were established in U.S. cities and one in Canada. Before this there were only six teams in the NHL.

The establishment of the World Hockey Association (WHA) in 1972 also has made hockey more popular in the United States. There are 12 teams in this new league. Eight of these teams are in U.S. cities.

Hockey has become more popular, too, because of television. Television coverage of the NHL games has drawn many new fans to the sport. People have found out that it's an exciting game to watch. Hockey is called the fastest game in the world, and it is also rough and dangerous.

Some long-time hockey fans believe that the game is not as well played now as it used to be. They complain that skaters who would never have gotten tryouts several years ago are now starting on the NHL and WHA expansion teams. These critics say the game is not exciting any more because the teams are not evenly matched in skill. Other fans argue that the expansion teams are good because they have given more skaters a chance to play the game. These fans believe that as the young players get experience, the teams will become evenly matched again.

This book is about 10 of the greatest scorers in the history of hockey. It is the play of these superstars that has given hockey its history. They have made it into the game it is today. Up to now, the history of hockey has been written mostly by Canadians. Some Canadian players, like Bobby Hull, Bobby Orr, Gordie Howe, Stan Mikita, Frank Mahovlich, and Phil Esposito, are familiar to sports fans in the United States. Others, like Maurice Richard, Bernie Geoffrion, Ted Lindsay, and Jean Beliveau, played their best years before hockey became popular in the United States.

A few players who may never rank among the leaders in scoring goals are also included in this

book. These players are important because they have gotten a lot of assists. And in hockey, scoring leadership is determined by both goals and assists. A player is given one point for each goal and one point for each assist he makes during a season. The goals and assists are then added together for total scoring points.

This small book can't begin to describe the colorful careers of these 10 hockey superstars. Their skating and playmaking has to be seen to be believed. But the book may give you an idea of what makes a player a superstar. All of these men have loved hockey and have played the game since they were children. Each of them practiced the game for years, aiming for a chance in the professional leagues. Pro hockey is a tough, hard-hitting game where players age quickly. It's hard to make it into the big leagues, and it's even harder to stay there. Each of these 10 men was not only able to stay in the game, but each also played brilliantly year after year.

Maurice Richard

Maurice Richard (mo-REES REE-shard) was the first superstar in the modern era of hockey. A great goal-getter, he had a quick shot that was usually right on the mark. Richard was always disappointed that he never won the NHL title for total points scored in a season. But he did score the most goals in a season five times during his 18-year NHL career.

Maurice Richard was born in Montreal, Quebec, in 1921. Like so many Canadian boys, he never wanted to be anything but a hockey player. During the long winters he practiced the game for hours, building strength in his ankles and legs. He even skated to and from school. Richard played in various leagues around Montreal until he was 19 years old. Then he was given a tryout with the Montreal Senior Royals, a farm team of the Montreal Canadiens. In his first game with the Royals, Richard broke an ankle. Because of this injury, he missed the rest of the season. The next year he played in only a few games before breaking a wrist. It seemed like Richard would never be healthy enough to get a chance in the professional league.

Finally, in 1942, Richard got a chance to play with the Montreal Canadiens. But his injury problem followed him. Early that year he broke an ankle again and sat out the rest of the season. In the 1943-44 season, Richard finally became free of major injuries. He began to live up to the promise that the Canadiens had seen in him. Playing at right wing in all but 4 of the 50 regular season games, Richard scored 32 goals and 22 assists. While his regular season play was outstanding that year, Richard's skating in the Stanley Cup playoffs was sensational. He scored 12 more goals in the playoff games—a record at that time. Five of those playoff goals came in one game against Toronto. They were the only goals that Montreal got in a 5-1 victory.

It was during the 1943-44 season that Richard picked up the nickname "Rocket" because of his tremendously hard shot. (When Maurice's brother, Henri, later joined the Canadiens, he was nicknamed "Pocket Rocket.") In the 1944-45 season, the Rocket's hard shots hit home game after game. That year Richard set a record that no one else has been able to match. He scored 50 goals in a 50-game season. Later on, after the number of games played in a season was increased, other players scored more than 50 goals in a season. But no one else in the modern era of hockey has ever averaged one goal a game for a season.

While on the ice, Richard only wanted to score

goals. He never believed in passing the puck for fancy plays. Instead, he simply held the puck on the blade of his stick and raced toward the net. If a defenseman got in his way, Richard held his stick in one hand and pushed his opponent away with the other.

Rocket Richard had a temper that was as quick as his speed on skates. In the 1954-55 season his temper got the better of him, and he gave a linesman a black eye. During the same game, he also gave a Boston Bruin player a tough beating. As a result, National Hockey League officials benched Richard for the rest of the year. This action started a riot by Montreal fans, who didn't like to see their favorite player out of action. After a tear gas bomb was thrown in the stadium, the fans rushed out into the streets. There, they broke windows, turned over cars, and looted stores. All in all, over $30,000 worth of damage was done that night in Montreal.

Richard retired in 1960 after 18 years in the NHL. He had led the Canadiens to eight Stanley Cup championships and to eight first-place finishes in the NHL. Richard had also set a career record of 544 goals in regular season play. Since then, that record has been broken by Gordie Howe.

One year after his retirement, Richard was elected to the Hockey Hall of Fame. A player is supposed to be retired for five years before he can be elected to the Hall of Fame. But this rule was overlooked for the Rocket, whom many hockey experts call the most exciting player ever to skate onto the ice.

Surrounded by the Montreal defense, Ted Lindsay fires one in for the Red Wings in the 1954 Stanley Cup playoffs.

Ted Lindsay

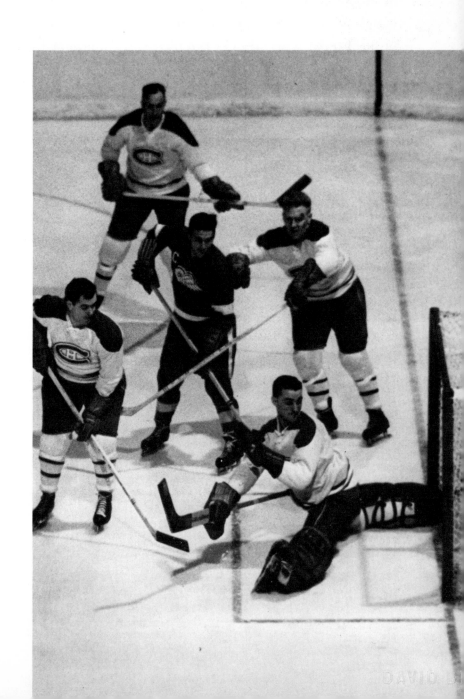

Ted Lindsay was the smallest of the great scorers in hockey. He stood 5 feet, 8 inches tall and weighed only 165 pounds. But despite his small build, Lindsay was one of the toughest men ever to skate in the NHL. His size never stopped him from battling any bigger player who checked him too hard.

Ted Lindsay was born in Renfrew, Ontario, in 1925. He was the youngest of five boys, and his father was a well-known Canadian hockey player. Ted learned early how to battle for the puck in family hockey games with his four older brothers. When he was a teen-ager, he went to school in Toronto. There he played Junior A hockey for two years before joining a minor-league professional team. Lindsay had only played a few months in the minor leagues when he was drafted by the Detroit Red Wings.

Lindsay joined the Red Wings at the beginning of the 1944-45 season. The 19-year-old rookie had a good year with 17 goals and 6 assists. The next season he got just 7 goals. But in the 1946-47 season, he became a scoring star with 27 goals. The following year, Lindsay began playing left wing on one of the greatest lines in the history of the game. Sid Abel was the center on the line, and Gordie Howe played wing opposite Lindsay. This line led the Red Wings to seven straight first-place finishes in the NHL, starting with the 1948-49 season. The Red Wings also won the Stanley Cup in four of those years.

During his career with Detroit, Lindsay was named the NHL's all-star left winger nine times. At the end of almost every season, he was in the running for the NHL scoring championship. In 1950, he took the championship with 23 goals and 55 assists. Although Lindsay got a lot of goals, he was never selfish with the puck. He was always a team player. He battled fiercely in the corners, digging out the puck to feed his teammates. Lindsay was also a scrappy player. He never knew what it was like to be a peaceful man on the ice. When an opponent checked Lindsay, he never ignored it. He always hit the man back—harder. In fact, it was amazing that Lindsay scored as much as he did, because he spent a lot of game time in the penalty box.

Lindsay had a happy career with Detroit until 1957. That year he helped start an NHL players' union. The Red Wings' management didn't approve of the union or of Lindsay's role in starting it. As a result, Lindsay was traded to the Chicago Black Hawks, even though he had just finished his best season ever—30 goals and 55 assists.

After playing three years with Chicago, Lindsay retired and went back to Detroit. There he became part-owner of a manufacturing company. But Lindsay soon missed skating, and he began to work out with the Red Wings in his free time. Before long, he decided that he would like to try his old career again. The Red Wings took Lindsay back on the team in 1964 when he was 39 years old. Some people criticized Lindsay's comeback. They said that a man of his age couldn't keep up with the younger players. Lindsay did have a slow start. But he finished the season with 14 goals and 14 assists to help the Red Wings take first place in the NHL. Lindsay then retired for good after a 17-year career in professional hockey.

In 1966 Lindsay was elected to the Hockey Hall of Fame. He finished his career as one of the 10 best scorers of all time, with 379 goals and 472 assists. Lindsay also left behind one other record—the 1,808 minutes he had served in the penalty box!

Bernie Geoffrion

Throughout his 14-year career with the Montreal Canadiens, Bernie Geoffrion (jeff-REE-own) played like a superstar. But for many of those years, Geoffrion never had the fame and glory of a superstar. This was because he started with the Canadiens when Maurice "Rocket" Richard was nearing the end of his career. Montreal's fans looked upon Richard as almost a god. They resented anyone who came close to playing as well as Richard. And Geoffrion did more than come close—he outplayed Richard a couple of seasons.

Bernie Geoffrion was born in Montreal, Quebec, in 1931. Even as a young boy, Geoffrion was a strong skater with a powerful shot. Because of these abilities, he was asked to join the Junior A league when he was only 14 years old. In Junior A hockey, Geoffrion played against boys who were two to six years older than he was. But Geoffrion was not afraid of skating against these more experienced players. He soon became a star in the Junior A league.

The Montreal Canadiens gave the teen-age star a tryout for a few games in the 1950-51 season. In his first professional game, Geoffrion suffered

Bernie Geoffrion (left) battles with a Red Wing opponent during the 1954 Stanley Cup playoffs.

one of his many career injuries. He slammed into a goal post, knocking out 14 teeth and breaking his nose. But Geoffrion recovered quickly. He rejoined the line-up and played so well that the Canadiens signed him. The 1951-52 season was Geoffrion's first full one with Montreal, and he had a great start. He scored 30 goals and 24 assists, and he was named the NHL's Rookie of the Year.

One of Geoffrion's greatest scoring seasons took place in 1954-55. At that time Geoffrion and his popular teammate Rocket Richard were battling for the goal-scoring title in the NHL. With only three games left in the season, Richard was leading when he was benched for hitting a referee. Geoffrion then passed up Richard's total points by one point and took the title. Scoring champions are usually heroes to the fans, but Geoffrion was not a hero to the Montreal fans. They booed him for outscoring their favorite player.

The Montreal fans booed Geoffrion again in 1961 when he tied Richard's season record of 50 goals. The fans did not believe this was a great accomplishment, because Geoffrion scored his 50 goals in a 70-game season. Richard had made his 50 goals when the team played only a 50-game season.

Despite the fans' jeers, Geoffrion kept playing

Diving for the puck, Geoffrion (Number 5) displays his tough playing style against the Boston Bruins.

and scoring. A strong shooter, Geoffrion stood only 5 feet, 9 inches tall, but he weighed 180 pounds. He was named "Boom-Boom" by the Montreal sportswriters. They called him this because of the sound made by his powerful slapshot when it hit the boards. He was one of the first and one of the best of the slapshooters.

Throughout his career, Geoffrion was bothered by injuries. One of his worst accidents took place during a team practice in 1959. Boom-Boom ran into a teammate and fell to the ice in great pain. When his pulse stopped beating for a short time, Geoffrion was rushed to a hospital. There he had emergency surgery for a ruptured internal organ. After missing 29 games, he returned to the Montreal line-up and helped the team win the Stanley Cup.

Geoffrion got another bad injury in a game against the Bruins during the 1963-64 season. He suffered a neck injury that damaged his vocal cords. Up to this time, Boom-Boom had hoped to have a singing career when he retired from hockey. He was such a good singer that he had appeared on many TV shows. But this accident ended Geoffrion's hopes for such a career.

Because of this neck injury, Geoffrion did not play much of the 1963-64 season, and he scored just 21 goals. Though he was only 33 years old, Geoffrion decided to retire. He then took a job coaching a Montreal farm team, the Quebec Aces. Geoffrion coached the Aces to two first-place finishes from 1964 to 1966. But the Aces lost out in the playoffs both times, and Boom-Boom was fired.

Geoffrion then announced that he wanted to make a comeback as a player. Montreal sold its rights to him to the New York Rangers, who wanted an older player to pull their team together. After playing two seasons with the Rangers, Boom-Boom became their head coach in 1968. But when he developed a stomach problem requiring surgery, he had to quit the coaching job. In 1972, a healthy Geoffrion returned to the NHL. He became head coach of the Atlanta Flames, an NHL expansion team. Geoffrion still held this job at the end of the 1973-74 season.

Jean Beliveau (zhan bell-i-VOE) probably came closest to being the most perfect hockey player ever to glide over the ice. He did everything well—skate, stickhandle, pass, and play defense. He was also an unselfish player who set up his teammates for goals.

Beliveau was born in Victoriaville, Quebec, in 1931. While growing up, his dream was to play for the Montreal Canadiens. As a boy, Beliveau did not look like a hockey player. He was quite tall and very thin. Fourteen-year-old Jean had the build of a basketball player when he began playing in the intermediate hockey leagues.

After scoring 42 goals in a single season with a Junior B team, Beliveau moved into the Quebec Junior A league, the last stop before the professional leagues. Beliveau soon became one of the best-known teen-age players in Canada. In his last season of Junior A, the young center scored 61 goals in only 43 games. After this achievement, he became a top prospect for the Montreal Canadiens, and they asked him to join their team. Although Beliveau had always wanted to play for the Canadiens, he turned them down. Instead, he signed with a senior amateur team in Quebec City. He was a hero in Quebec City, and he was making more money there than he would in the NHL.

The only way Montreal could get Beliveau was to

buy the whole Quebec senior amateur league. The Canadiens had to get the rights to every player in the league and then change the league from amateur to professional status. And that's just what Montreal did to get Beliveau. It turned out to be a good move for the Canadiens.

When Beliveau joined Montreal in 1953, the team was stacked with superstars. These stars included "Rocket" Richard, "Boom-Boom" Geoffrion, Dickie Moore, and Doug Harvey. Injuries kept Beliveau from playing his whole first season with the Canadiens. He finished with just 13 goals and 21 assists. But the next year he got 37 goals and 36 assists. The 6-foot, 3-inch, 210-pound Beliveau had begun to take his place among the other superstars on his team.

Starting with the 1955-56 season, Montreal won five straight Stanley Cup playoffs. In regular season play before the first of these wins, Beliveau led the NHL in scoring. He had 47 goals and 41 assists. Through the years, Beliveau became the quiet leader of the Canadiens—the man the team looked to when things went bad. He seemed at his best in tough games. When Beliveau was out of the line-up because of injuries, Montreal often seemed to slump. But the team's spirit picked up again when the big center returned.

Beliveau had that magic quality of leadership that can drive teams to great achievements. He played 17 seasons with the Canadiens. During those years they won the Stanley Cup playoffs 10 times. One of the greatest of these playoff wins took place in Beliveau's last season. That was the 1970-71 season, when Montreal upset the powerful Boston Bruins. Beliveau, then 40 years old, finished fourth in playoff scoring with 6 goals and 16 assists.

After the last 1971 playoff game, Beliveau announced that he was going to hang up his hockey skates for good. He got hundreds of letters from fans, asking him not to quit. His teammates also asked him to keep playing. But Beliveau wanted to quit while a winner. He also wished to spend more time with his family. In the end, Beliveau wound up staying with the Canadiens anyway, but as a businessman, not as a player. The owners of the Canadiens thought as much of Beliveau's abilities off the ice as on. They made him vice president of a company that they owned.

Great stars come and go quickly in professional hockey. It may be a while, though, before the game sees another player with the all-around ability of Jean Beliveau.

Bobby Orr

Success came to Bobby Orr early in his professional career. After only three years in the NHL, the 21-year-old Orr had won every award available to a defenseman. He even took some of these awards two or three times in a row. Unless injuries end his career early, Orr probably will leave behind a string of successes unequalled in the game.

Bobby Orr was born in Parry Sound, Ontario, in 1948. He began playing organized hockey before he was old enough to go to school. By the time he was 12 years old, National Hockey League scouts were interested in Bobby. The Boston Bruins finally beat out all the other clubs that wanted to sign the young defenseman. When he was only 14 years old, Orr agreed to play on the Boston Bruins' Junior A team, the Oshawa Generals. It was a compliment to Orr's ability that the Bruins gave him a chance in Junior A hockey that early. Usually, Junior A hockey is played only by boys who are 16 to 20 years old.

Orr's parents wanted him to live at home until he was at least 15 years old. So, several times a week, Orr made a 350-mile round trip between his hometown and Oshawa for games. When Orr first told the coach of the Oshawa Generals that he played defense, his older teammates laughed. At that time, Orr was not much more than 5 feet, 2 inches tall, and he weighed only 110 pounds. He did not look big enough to be a defenseman, especially one who would have to compete against boys older than he.

But Orr's new teammates did not laugh long. Orr soon became the star of the Junior A league. Whenever he was on the ice, he controlled the game. His older teammates began to look for him to start most of the plays. This was because of Orr's unusual way of playing defense. A defenseman is not counted on to score goals. Instead, he usually carries the puck only a short distance before feeding it to the center or to one of the wings. Then he skates back to defend his goalie against the other team. But Orr has never played that kind of defense. If there is an open man, Orr passes the puck to him. But Orr also carries the puck deep into the other team's zone to score. Even though he does this often, he's seldom caught out of his defensive position when the other team starts back up the ice.

This kind of a defenseman with scoring ability was just what the Boston Bruins needed. For several years, the Bruins had been one of the lowest scoring teams in the NHL. As soon as Orr turned 18 and became old enough to play in the NHL, the Bruins brought him up. Orr more than fulfilled the Bruins' hopes. In 1966-67, his first season, Orr got

13 goals and 28 assists. He finished the season on a high note, earning Rookie of the Year honors. The next season, his scoring dropped off after he injured a knee. But even so, he was voted the outstanding defenseman in the NHL that year.

Bobby Orr (Number 4) assists in defending a Bruin goal against the Montreal Canadiens.

By the 1968-69 season, Orr was healthy again. On his 21st birthday—March 20, 1969—Orr scored his 21st goal of the season. With this goal, he broke the NHL record for goals scored by a defenseman. That record had been standing since 1945. Orr finished the season with a total of 64 points—a new point record for defensemen.

In the years that followed, the Bruins put together one of the best teams in NHL history, with the great Bobby Orr as their leader. In the 1969-70 season, the Bruins won the Stanley Cup for the first time in 29 years. Orr's play that season was almost beyond belief. He led the NHL in scoring with 33 goals and 87 assists. As a result, he was chosen the Most Valuable Player in the league. As great as he was that season, Orr was even better during the 1970-71 season. He scored 37 goals and 102 assists. No other player, before or since, has come close to getting 102 assists in a single season. In the 1971-72 season, the Bruins again won the Stanley Cup. They took it in a tough, six-game series against the New York Rangers. Although Orr had another knee injury, he led the Bruins to the win.

Because he was recovering from knee surgery, Orr joined the Bruins after they were 15 games into the 1972-73 season. But despite his late start, Orr scored 101 points—29 goals and 72 assists—in

63 games. He finished third in total season scoring in the league. And for the sixth year in a row, he was named the best defenseman in the NHL. The Bruins went on to meet the New York Rangers in the opening round of the Stanley Cup playoffs, but the Rangers took them in only five games. The Bruins' coach was disappointed in his team's play. He said that Bobby Orr had been Boston's only real hockey player in the series against the Rangers.

The same thing happened in the 1973-74 Stanley Cup playoffs. The Philadelphia Flyers beat Boston in all but two games. Many sports writers felt that those two games were won by Boston because of Orr's great performance. In the 1973-74 season, Orr got 32 goals and 90 assists. This brought his career total to 735 points in 541 games. Orr was also named best NHL defenseman for the seventh straight year.

Hockey experts believe that Orr may go down in the game's history as the greatest player of all time —if he can stay healthy. Since his first NHL season, Orr has had several operations on his left knee. None of these operations has been completely successful, and Orr has played many games in great pain. But because of his determination to stay in the game despite injury, Orr probably will keep playing for years to come.

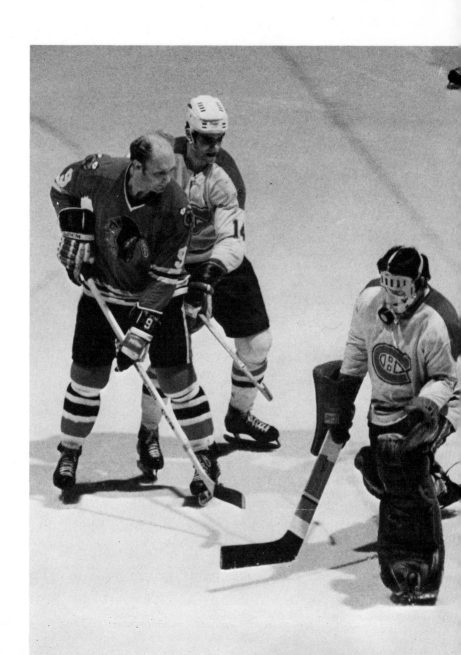

Many hockey experts call Bobby Hull the best offensive player the game has ever known in its history. Nicknamed the "Golden Jet" because of his blond hair and fast skating, the strong left winger has the build of a weight lifter. He shoots the puck as though it were fired out of a cannon. Opposing players often foul Hull to stop him from scoring, but he rarely hits back. Hull has always been an easy-going, gentle man.

Bobby Hull was born in the small town of Point Anne, Ontario, in 1939. An older sister taught him how to skate when he was 4 years old. She was a good teacher. When Hull was only 11 years old, he was spotted by a scout for the Chicago Black Hawks. He was playing for a bantam hockey team at the time. Three years later, he signed with Chicago and moved 170 miles away to play for a Black Hawks farm team.

The Hawks brought Hull into the NHL in 1957, when he was 18 years old. He got only 13 goals that season and just 18 the next. But in 1959-60, his third season, Hull took the NHL scoring championship with 39 goals and 42 assists. In the 1960-61 season, Hull and his teammate Stan Mikita led the Black Hawks to a Stanley Cup win. It was the Hawks' first NHL championship in 23 years. The next season, when he was just 23 years old, Hull scored 50 goals. At that time, only two other players had scored 50 goals in a season. Hull broke that record with 54 goals in the 1965-66 season. The next year, he got 52 goals. That was also the year he led the Black Hawks to a first-place finish in the NHL. It was the first time in their 40-year history that the Hawks had led the NHL at the end of the regular season.

At the start of the 1969-70 season, Hull had a contract dispute with Chicago. Because of this, he missed the first 14 games of the season. He received a lot of criticism from the fans and the sportswriters for not playing. The criticism hurt Hull, and it was one of the reasons that he jumped from the NHL to the new World Hockey Association in 1972. The other reason was money. To draw away some of the superstars from the NHL, the WHA offered huge sums of money. The Winnipeg Jets of the WHA offered $3 million to Hull for a five-year contract. Hull took the offer. As player-coach of Winnipeg, Hull led the Jets to first place in the western division of the WHA in the 1972-73 season. But the Jets lost to the New England Whalers in the WHA championship playoffs.

Except for signing that huge contract with Winnipeg, Hull's greatest moment in hockey probably came on March 25, 1972. That was when he

knocked in the 600th goal of his NHL career. Only Gordie Howe has scored more goals than that. Hull went on to end the 1973-74 season with 53 goals and 42 assists. If he continues to perform as well as he has so far, he may overtake Howe's lifetime NHL record of 786 goals.

Hull has always been a great goal-getter because of his speed. Goalies have been known to duck when Hull races down the ice and raises his stick to slap a shot. The puck comes off his stick so fast that it's just a blur in the air. The goalies have a right to be afraid of Hull's slapshot. Some of them have been hit by his hard shots and knocked unconscious, even when wearing face masks.

Hockey experts were so amazed by Hull's fast skating and quick slapshots that they measured their speeds. It was learned that Hull was the fastest man in the NHL when skating with the puck. He traveled just under 30 miles an hour. His slapshot was timed at just over 118 miles an hour. This is about 35 miles an hour faster than the average for all the players in the NHL.

Despite his superstar status, Hull has changed very little from the boy who grew up in tiny Point Anne. He is one of those rare stars who has never refused a sportswriter's request for an interview. And he has never turned down anyone who asks for his autograph.

In the off-season, Hull and his family live on a farm near Millbrook, Ontario. When Hull puts aside his hockey stick for good, he probably will retire to his farm and raise Hereford cattle.

Gordie Howe was the greatest scorer in the history of the NHL. He was also one of the toughest and meanest players in the league. Opposing players usually stayed clear of Howe on the ice, even when he had the puck. They were afraid to check the big right winger because they knew he would get even with them in a way that hurt.

Gordie Howe was born in Floral, Saskatchewan, in 1928. One of eight children, Howe began playing organized hockey when he was nine years old. Hockey was more important than school to Howe, who was a quiet boy with few friends. Even when the temperature dropped to 40 degrees below zero, he skated on an outside rink. He quit high school after his first year and went to a New York Rangers camp in Winnipeg. But he returned home when the Rangers told him that he would never make it in the NHL. They said he was too clumsy on the ice.

Howe did not let the Rangers' criticism of his skating discourage him. He continued to play the game he loved. It was when he was playing in a church hockey league that Howe was spotted by the Detroit Red Wings. They asked him to come to their camp. This time he made the team and stayed. In fact, Howe stayed with the Red Wings for 25 years. And in that time, he broke more NHL records and won more trophies than any other player in the history of the game.

Howe did not have a great start with the Red Wings. Playing at right wing, he got only 7 goals in 1946-47, his first season. He scored just 16 goals in his second season and 12 in his third. But then the points started to come, and they came fast. By the end of the 1950-51 season, Howe had scored over 100 goals. In the 1952-53 season, he made his 200th goal. Howe scored number 300 in the 1955-56 season and number 400 two years later. In the 1961-62 season, he boosted his total to over 400 goals.

Howe's most important goal was scored on November 10, 1963. On that day he made the 545th goal of his career. That goal broke the career record set by the great Maurice "Rocket" Richard. It was scored against Richard's old team, the Montreal Canadiens. Not counting playoff goals, Howe scored 786 goals in his NHL career— the highest total in the history of the game.

Howe was able to score so many goals because of his strong, quick shot. With a snap of his wrists, he could send a puck flying along at 114 miles an hour. He played with a 21-ounce stick—the heaviest stick used by any player in the NHL. Ordinary hockey sticks broke in his powerful hands.

The big right wing always played a strong, reckless kind of hockey that resulted in many injuries. His worst injury came in a Stanley Cup playoff game against the Toronto Maple Leafs in 1950. Skating fast, Howe went in to check a Maple Leaf player. But the player stepped away from Howe, and the right winger crashed headfirst into the boards. As a result, Howe's skull, cheekbones, and nose were fractured. He also got cuts on one eye. Very close to death, Howe was taken to a hospital. There he had brain surgery that saved his life. He was let out of the hospital in time to see the Red Wings win the Stanley Cup. After the last game, his teammates handed the trophy to Howe to carry off the ice.

The season after this accident, Howe was back at right wing for Detroit, just as mean as ever. In fact, some opposing players claimed that the 6-foot, 205-pound wing became even tougher after his almost-fatal injury. Howe went on playing year after year, even though injuries piled on top of injuries. He suffered a second serious blow to his head, cracked his ribs three times, and broke a wrist. He also had operations on both knees and got cuts on his face requiring over 300 stitches. But Howe kept playing through all of this as though age would never catch up with him. In the 1968-69

Gordie Howe (far left) and his Red Wing teammates get into the action against the Montreal Canadiens (1969).

season, when he was 40 years old, he scored 44 goals and 59 assists—one of his best seasons ever.

It seemed as though Howe would never quit the game he loved. But after the 1970-71 season, during which he scored 23 goals, Howe retired from the Red Wings. He was 43 years old, and he had played more seasons in the NHL than any other player. Howe then took a job with the Red Wings' management. But he didn't stay off the ice for long.

Howe had often said that he wanted to play on the same team with his two boys, Marty and Mark. In 1973, he got the chance to do just that. All three Howes signed with the Houston Aeros, a WHA team. Playing for the Aeros, Gordie Howe finished off the 1973-74 season with 31 goals and 69 assists. He was named the WHA's Most Valuable Player of 1974. Howe's son Mark was chosen as the WHA's 1974 Rookie of the Year. It seems as though hockey will always be a way of life for all of the Howes.

Stan Mikita (meh-KEY-tah) became a superstar in the NHL even though some of his best years were played in the shadow of his famous teammate Bobby Hull. While both men were with the Chicago Black Hawks, Hull got most of the publicity and cheers from the fans. But hockey experts knew that Mikita was not "number two" to anyone in all-around playing ability.

Mikita was born Stan Gvoth in Czechoslovakia in 1940. His parents were poor, and they decided their son would have a better life in Canada. So when Stan was eight years old, he was sent to St. Catherines, Ontario. There he was adopted by an aunt and uncle, and he took their last name. At first, the young Czech had a hard time in the new country. Everything was new and strange, especially the language. Other children made fun of him because he couldn't speak English. Although Stan had trouble with the new language, he had no trouble learning how to play a new game— hockey. A neighbor boy showed Mikita how to play hockey by using sign language. "Stick" and "puck" were two of the first English words that Stan learned.

Even as a boy, Mikita was an outstanding hockey player. He was also a scrappy player. Since Mikita was small, his bigger opponents usually tried to knock him around. But Mikita never backed away from a fight. Often he traded punches with boys who were 30 to 40 pounds heavier than he was. In high school, Mikita became a top athlete in hockey, baseball, football, and basketball. In fact, he became such a good catcher that he got an offer from a professional baseball team. But he turned it down because of his love for hockey.

When he was 17 years old, Mikita joined the TeePees, a Junior A team owned by the Black Hawks. He became an outstanding center with the TeePees, and in the 1958-59 season, he took the league scoring title with 97 points. After this great scoring season, the Black Hawks signed Mikita and brought him into the NHL. The small, scrappy center didn't have a strong start. He got just 8 goals and 18 assists in the 1959-60 season. But he did get a lot of penalty time—119 minutes—because he fought back whenever he was fouled.

From his second season on, Mikita began to establish himself as one of the great scorers in the NHL. In the 1963-64 season, only his fifth in the league, Mikita led the NHL in scoring with 39 goals and 50 assists. That was the first of four scoring titles he won. Meanwhile, Mikita also became known as a tough little player who wouldn't take a lot of knocking around without trying to get even. Mikita stood 5 feet, 9 inches tall, but he weighed only 165 pounds. He was too small to fight back with body checks. However, his bigger opponents soon learned to stay away from Mikita's slashing stick.

In the 1966-67 season Mikita stopped being the angry little center. That year he got only 12 penalty minutes. Mikita said that he decided to stop his rough playing as he sat in the penalty box one night. He realized that he was missing chances to score whenever he got a penalty. Mikita changed so much that he won the trophy given to the most gentlemanly player in the league in 1967. That year he was also the NHL's top point-getter and most valuable player. He became the first player ever to win three major awards in one season. And the next season, he won all three awards again.

In the 1970-71 season, Mikita's scoring dropped off. He got only 24 goals and 48 assists. Some people said that he had lost his competitive spirit. But there was more to it than that. In a 1969 game, Mikita suffered a back injury that bothered him for the next two seasons. By the 1972-73 season, his back was finally better, and Mikita began to score again. But then he chipped an ankle bone and missed 21 games. Mikita was able to play in 57 games, however, and he finished the season

Stan Mikita's shot sails past the Montreal goalie in a 1972 Black Hawk-Canadien battle.

with 27 goals and 56 assists. He then picked up 20 more points in the Stanley Cup playoffs. During the 1973-74 season, Mikita got 30 goals and 50 assists. This brought his career total to 1,154 points in 1,052 games.

Since joining the Black Hawks, Mikita has gone to Czechoslovakia several times to see his mother and father. On a 1967 visit to his homeland, he worked with young Czech hockey players. Mikita had a lot to teach them. He has always been considered one of the best stickhandlers in hockey, as well as one of the best players in all-around ability.

Mikita will also be remembered in hockey history for something that will not show up in the record books. He was the first player to use a curved stick. A puck shot off a curved stick turns and spins through the air. This makes it hard for a goalie to judge where the puck will land. Most players in the NHL started using the curved stick after Stan Mikita introduced it.

Frank Mahovlich

It's unusual when the play of a superstar is criticized by the hometown fans. But this kind of criticism has played a big part in the career of Frank Mahovlich (ma-HAV-lich). It seemed as if no matter how well he played, the fans always expected more of him.

Frank Mahovlich was born in Timmins, Ontario, in 1938. He played hockey all through his childhood, as did his younger brother, Pete. It was when Frank played for a Toronto high school team that he became a promising professional prospect. At that time, the Toronto Maple Leafs were looking for a strong offensive player to help bring them out of a slump. Everyone in Toronto thought that Mahovlich, nicknamed the "Big M," would be that player. At the beginning of the 1956-57 season, the Maple Leafs called up the schoolboy star for a try-out. But Mahovlich did not make the team.

A year later, Mahovlich did make the Toronto team. He had an excellent rookie season in 1957-58, scoring 20 goals. That was the same year that the great Bobby Hull also broke into the NHL. Because of his top goal-scoring, Mahovlich beat out the "Golden Jet" for rookie-of-the-year honors. But this victory over Hull was to hurt the Big M over the next few years. The Toronto fans expected Mahovlich always to do as well as Hull in scoring.

For the next two seasons, Mahovlich continued to play good hockey with the Maple Leafs. But the team still fell short of becoming a winning club. Mahovlich alone was not enough to change the team's bad playing. However, some people began to put all the blame for the team's losses on Mahovlich. The sportswriters and the fans complained that the Big M wasn't scoring enough. The Toronto coach said that he was disappointed in Mahovlich's play. Because of the criticism he got from all sides, Mahovlich became moody and silent. He refused to give interviews and did not talk to his teammates.

But despite the criticism, the Big M kept playing his best. He had a great year in the 1960-61 season, getting 48 goals and 36 assists. He then led Toronto to three straight Stanley Cup championships, from 1962 through 1964. But even these wins didn't stop criticism of the 6-foot, 200-pound left winger. The Toronto sportswriters still found fault with his play, and he did not get along with the Maple Leafs' coach.

When Mahovlich's scoring dropped off in the 1964-65 season, the fans forgot about the three championships and began to boo him every time he stepped on the ice. It was then that Mahovlich had a nervous breakdown. The doctors said it was because of all the criticism he had received.

Mahovlich suffered another breakdown during the 1967-68 season. Finally, the management of the Maple Leafs did the best thing they could for the Big M. They traded him to the Detroit Red Wings in March 1968.

At Detroit, Mahovlich was put on the same line with two other great players, Gordie Howe and Alex Delvecchio. With the pressure off him finally, Mahovlich began to change. He started talking to the other players, and he became a happy man. In 1968-69 he had one of his greatest seasons, scoring 49 goals and 29 assists. But Mahovlich's happy days at Detroit ended soon. During the 1970-71 season the management of the Red Wings had problems, and the team was broken up.

In January 1971, Mahovlich was traded to the Montreal Canadiens. Montreal fans have been known to be as critical of their star players as the Toronto fans. It might have been a bad trade for Mahovlich, but two things stopped this from happening. In the first place, Frank's younger brother, Pete, had been with the Canadiens for two years and was a popular player. Because of Pete, the Montreal fans were friendly toward Frank right away. And more important, Mahovlich got off to a good start, scoring 17 goals and 24 assists in what was left of the regular season. At the end of that season, the Canadiens upset the Boston Bruins to win the Stanley Cup. During the playoff games, Mahovlich set a record of 14 goals. Seven of those goals were scored against the Bruins.

At the start of the 1971-72 season, the Montreal

sportswriters began to criticize Mahovlich. But he quieted his critics by getting 43 goals and 53 assists to lead Montreal in scoring. Mahovlich had another fine season in 1972-73, getting 38 goals and 55 assists. The Canadiens also won the Stanley Cup that season. Mahovlich finished up the 1973-74 season with 31 goals and 49 assists. This brought his career total to 533 goals and 570 assists.

Today Mahovlich is a confident man who has earned a place among hockey's all-time greats. His critics can't take that away from the Big M now, no matter what he does in the coming years.

Phil Esposito

Of all the great scoring stars still playing in the NHL, Phil Esposito (es-poe-ZEE-toe) has the best chance to break Gordie Howe's career record of goals scored. But even if he does not break Howe's record, Esposito already has set records that probably will stand for many years.

Phil Esposito was born in 1942 in Sault Ste. Marie, Ontario. Unlike many of hockey's other superstars, Esposito did not win early fame. He worked his way through Canadian Junior B hockey before making it into the Junior A league when he was 19 years old. By that age, any young player showing promise usually has been given a chance on an NHL team. But Esposito did not get his chance for almost another two years. Meanwhile, he played on a team in the minor professional leagues.

Finally, Esposito was called up by the Chicago Black Hawks in the 1963-64 season. The 6-foot, 1-inch, 210-pound center got only 3 goals and 2 assists in 27 games that season. At the start of the 1964-65 season, the Black Hawks put Esposito on a line with Bobby Hull, the "Golden Jet." During the three years Esposito played on that line, he became an excellent playmaker, feeding the goal

Phil Esposito (Number 7) holds off his Canadien opponent as he fights for a good shooting position.

to Hull's powerful slapshot. Because of Esposito's steady passing, Hull led the NHL in goal-scoring all three years. Meanwhile, Esposito totaled up scores of 23, 27, and 21 goals during those same three seasons.

Just before the 1967-68 season, the Black Hawks sent Esposito, Ken Hodge, and Fred Stanfield to the Boston Bruins. In return, the Hawks got Gil Marotte, Pit Martin, and Jack Norris. It proved to be a bad trade for Chicago and a good one for Boston. Although Chicago lost one Esposito, they soon got another one. Phil's younger brother, Tony, became a star goalie with the Black Hawks.

After joining the Bruins, Esposito began to play like a superstar. He finished the 1967-68 season with 35 goals and a league-leading 49 assists. In the 1968-69 season, Esposito fired in 49 goals and got 77 assists for a total of 126 points. That was the greatest season scoring record that any NHL player had ever achieved up to that time. At the end of the season, Esposito was voted Most Valuable Player in the league.

The 1970-71 season was Esposito's greatest on the ice. The big center scored 76 goals in 78 games. That was 18 goals more than the old season record of 58 set by Esposito's former teammate Bobby Hull. In the same season, Esposito also had 76 assists, for a total of 152 points. Both of those records may stand for years.

Esposito often scores from an area close to the opponents' net. He stands about 20 feet in front of the net. Then he dares his opponents to move him out of there. But Esposito's size and strength make it hard for them to move him. Suddenly, one of his wings will throw the puck into his area. Then, with a quick movement of his stick, Esposito gets a shot off.

While Esposito was setting NHL scoring records, many people were criticizing his goal-getting ability. They said that Esposito would not have scored so much if the NHL had not expanded, bringing in so many young players. They claimed that it was easy for Esposito to score against new and inexperienced players. Other people said that Esposito's scoring increased because he was playing on the same line with Bobby Orr. They said that opponents could not watch both of these players closely and keep them from scoring.

But Esposito's play in the 1972 series between Team Canada and the national Soviet hockey team quieted many of these critics. Team Canada took the Soviets in the best of eight series. Esposito became the leader of Team Canada, which was made up of stars from all of the NHL teams. He

Esposito (Number 7) takes the Bruin offensive against the Canadiens in a 1969 match.

played in all eight games against the Soviets, scoring a total of 7 goals and 6 assists. Esposito scored all of these points as a member of a line that did not include Bobby Orr. (Orr was recovering from knee surgery.) And more important, Esposito's goals were scored against experienced players, not newcomers to the game. Because of his great play in this series, Esposito was named Canadian Athlete of the Year in 1972.

The other players in the NHL have always been aware of Esposito's talents. In 1971 he won the first Lester B. Pearson trophy. This trophy is given to the player voted most outstanding by all the other players in the NHL. That same year, the NHL's coaches voted Esposito the best stickhandler in the game.

Esposito continued to be a top goal-getter in the 1972-73 season. He got a total of 130 points—55 goals and 75 assists. As a result, he won the NHL scoring title—his fourth scoring title in five years.

In the 1973-74 season, Esposito again led the league in scoring, with 69 goals and 77 assists. He was also named Most Valuable Player in the NHL. Esposito ended the season with a career record of 466 goals and 577 assists. With a total of 1,043 points, he was the youngest hockey player ever to become a member of the exclusive "1,000-point club." Esposito still has many good years of hockey left. If he keeps scoring as much as he has been, he may overtake Gordie Howe's lifetime NHL record of 786 goals before his playing days end.

About the Author

Richard Rainbolt is a longtime sports fan who has written a number of lively, well-received sports books. Among them are *Gold Glory*, a history of the Minnesota Gophers; *The Goldy Shuffle*, the story of Bill Goldsworthy of the Minnesota North Stars; and *The Minnesota Vikings*, a fast-paced history of that famous team. As one might guess from his books, the author is a native of Minnesota. After serving in the U.S. Marines, Mr. Rainbolt attended the University of Minnesota, where he received a degree in journalism. Since then, he has worked as a newspaper reporter, a public relations man, and a reporter for the Associated Press. In addition to writing, Mr. Rainbolt now runs his own public relations firm.